EARTH**ROCKS!**
GLACIERS
BY SARA GILBERT

CREATIVE EDUCATION • CREATIVE PAPERBACKS

Published by Creative Education and Creative Paperbacks
P.O. Box 227, Mankato, Minnesota 56002
Creative Education and Creative Paperbacks are
imprints of The Creative Company
www.thecreativecompany.us

Design and production by Chelsey Luther
Art direction by Rita Marshall
Printed in the United States of America

Photographs by Dreamstime (Carlos Ameglio, TMarchev), Getty
Images (The Asahi Shimbun, Danita Delimont, Jason Edwards,
KEENPRESS, Andy Rouse, Spaces Images, Punnawit Suwuttananun,
Steve Whiston – Fallen Log Photography), iStockphoto (Dash_med,
elnavegante, lucentius), National Geographic Creative (WILD
WONDERS OF EUROPE/LIODDEN/NATUREPL.COM), Spoon Graphics
(Chris Spooner)

Library of Congress Cataloging-in-Publication Data
Names: Gilbert, Sara.
Title: Glaciers / Sara Gilbert.
Series: Earth Rocks!
Includes bibliographical references and index.
Summary: An elementary exploration of glaciers, focusing on the
geological evidence that helps explain how and where they form and
spotlighting famous examples, such as those in Glacier National Park.
Identifiers: ISBN 978-1-60818-894-9 (hardcover) / ISBN 978-1-62832-
510-2 (pbk) / ISBN 978-1-56660-946-3 (eBook)

This title has been submitted for CIP processing under
LCCN 2017937620.

CCSS: RI.1.1, 2, 4, 5, 6, 7; RI.2.2, 5, 6, 7, 10; RI.3.1, 5, 7, 8; RF.1.1, 3, 4; RF.2.3, 4

First Edition HC 9 8 7 6 5 4 3 2 1
First Edition PBK 9 8 7 6 5 4 3 2 1

Pictured on cover: **Perito Moreno Glacier, Argentina (top)**

TABLE OF CONTENTS

CRACKED ICE

There is a mountain of ice ahead of you. You can hear it creaking and cracking. Then, a *boom*! A chunk of ice has broken off. The glacier has changed again!

ICE ON THE MOVE

Glaciers are huge masses of tightly packed ice. They have many cracks and **crevasses**.

Glaciers are always moving. They pick up rocks, sticks, and other **debris** as they slowly slide across the earth. They usually move about three feet (0.9 m) a day.

ANCIENT ICE

It can take hundreds of years for a glacier to form. Ice and snow pile up and get pushed together very tightly.

Glaciers often look blue. This is because all the air bubbles are squeezed out. Newer glaciers are usually whiter.

alpine glacier

GORNER GLACIER

ice sheet

GREENLAND ICE SHEET

ice cap

AUSTFONNA POLAR ICE CAP

ICE UP HIGH

Alpine glaciers form on mountaintops. Very large glaciers are called ice sheets. Smaller ice sheets are called ice caps.

CHANGING SHAPE

Glaciers can be found on every **continent** but Australia. As the world gets warmer, glaciers change, too. Warmer temperatures make the ice melt more quickly.

GOING TO THE GLACIERS

The largest glacier in the world is in Antarctica. It is 250 miles (402 km) long and 60 miles (96.6 km) wide.

GRINNELL GLACIER, MONTANA

It can be hard to visit Antarctica, though. It would be easier to go to Glacier National Park in Montana. There are 25 glaciers there!

ACTIVITY: MOVING LIKE A GLACIER

Materials

Two colors of Play-Doh

Pebbles and small sticks

Rolling pin

1. Put one container of Play-Doh in the refrigerator to make it cold.

2. Roll the other Play-Doh out to make a smooth, flat surface.

3. Gently place the pebbles and other items on the smooth Play-Doh.

4. Mold the cold Play-Doh into a ball, and place it at one end of the smooth surface. That will be your glacier.

5. Slowly drag your "glacier" across the surface. Does it pick up the pebbles and sticks? What happens to the smooth surface as you keep moving the glacier across it?

GLOSSARY

alpine: relating to high mountains

continent: one of the seven main landmasses on Earth

crevasses: deep cracks in a glacier

debris: loose natural materials, including rocks, dirt, and leaves

READ MORE

Mis, Melody S. *Exploring Glaciers*. New York: PowerKids Press, 2009.

Simon, Seymour. *Icebergs and Glaciers*. New York: HarperCollins, 1999.

WEBSITES

National Geographic Kids: Glacier Facts

http://www.ngkids.co.uk/science-and-nature/Glaciers

Learn more about glaciers and see stunning pictures, too!

Science Kids Earth Facts: Glacier Facts for Kids

http://www.sciencekids.co.nz/sciencefacts/earth/glaciers.html

Learn interesting facts about glaciers.

Note: Every effort has been made to ensure that any websites listed above were active at the time of publication and suitable for children. However, because of the nature of the Internet, it is impossible to guarantee that these sites will remain active indefinitely or that their contents will not be altered.

INDEX